READY, SET, GAME!

HANDHELD GAMING

BY BETSY RATHBURN

TORQUE™

TM

TORQUE brims with excitement
perfect for thrill-seekers of all kinds.
Discover daring survival skills, explore
uncharted worlds, and marvel at mighty
engines and extreme sports. In *Torque* books,
anything can happen. Are you ready?

This edition first published in 2021 by Bellwether Media, Inc.

No part of this publication may be reproduced in whole or in part without
written permission of the publisher. For information regarding permission,
write to Bellwether Media, Inc., Attention: Permissions Department,
6012 Blue Circle Drive, Minnetonka, MN 55343.

Library of Congress Cataloging-in-Publication Data

LC record for Handheld Gaming available at https://lccn.loc.gov/2020048065

Editor: Elizabeth Neuenfeldt   Designer: Brittany McIntosh

Printed in the United States of America, North Mankato, MN.

TABLE OF CONTENTS

SKATE CITY

You choose your favorite skateboard.
Time to ride! You kick off by touching the
screen. *Skate City* lets you skateboard on
your smartphone!

The city blurs as you speed past buildings and people. You **grind** down a curb and race to the next **obstacle**. This handheld game is a fun way to skate!

MORE MOBILE SKATING

In 2019, *Tony Hawk's Skate Jam* was released on smartphones. This skateboarding game is based on the popular Tony Hawk's Pro Skater games!

4m

HANDHELD GAMING
HISTORY

Auto Race

Handheld gaming started in 1976. A company called Mattel released *Auto Race*. It was a simple device with a small screen. Its only noises were beeps.

The car was a light. Players used two switches to control the light's movements and speed. They avoided obstacles as they raced!

HANDHELD GAMING TIMELINE

1976
Auto Race is the first handheld game

1979
Milton Bradley Microvision is the first handheld game device to use cartridges

1984
Epoch Game Pocket Computer is released in Japan

1989
Nintendo Game Boy is released

1998
Game Boy Color is released with a color screen

2004
PlayStation Portable is released

2004
Nintendo DS is the first handheld game device with a touchscreen

2011
A new version of the Playstation Portable, PlayStation Vita, is released

2017
Nintendo Switch is released

In 1979, the Milton Bradley Microvision was released. It was the first handheld game system to use **cartridges**. Players could switch between many games!

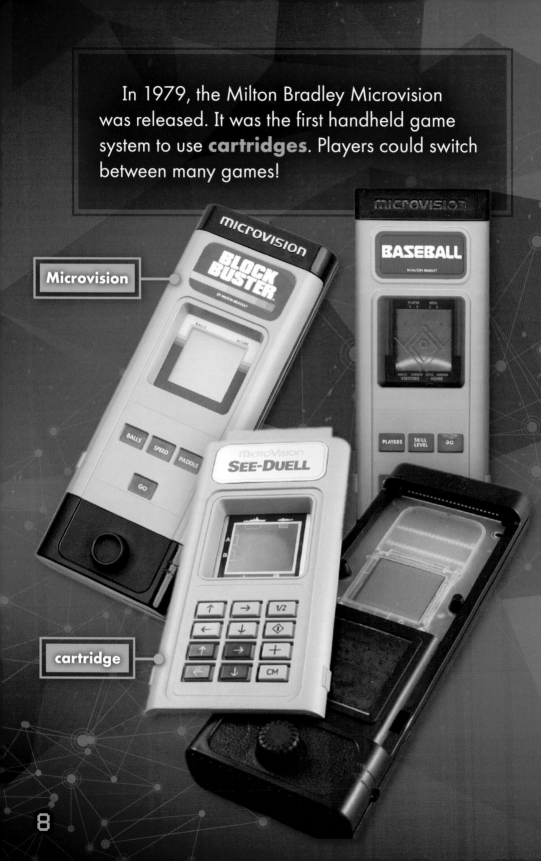

Microvision

cartridge

Epoch Game Pocket Computer

Nintendo Game & Watch

The 1980s brought many different handheld game systems. Nintendo's Game & Watch devices were popular. The 1984 Epoch Game Pocket Computer was only released in Japan. But its technology paved the way for future handheld devices.

The earliest handheld game systems were too expensive for most people. In 1989, the Nintendo Game Boy was released. It cost almost half the price of similar devices.

The Game Boy had a green screen with black **graphics**. It came with *Tetris*. Other favorite games were *Kirby's Dream Land* and *Pokémon Red* and *Blue*.

NOW IN COLOR!

The Game Boy Color came out in 1998. It had a color screen!

Kirby's Dream Land

HANDHELD NINTENDO GAMING THROUGH TIME

1989
Game Boy

1998
Game Boy
Color

2001
Game Boy
Advance

2003
Game Boy
Advance SP

2004
Nintendo DS

2005
Game Boy Micro

2011
Nintendo 3DS

2013
Nintendo 2DS

2017
Nintendo
Switch

2019
Nintendo Switch
Lite

Nintendo DS

stylus

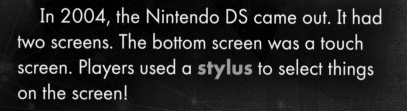

In 2004, the Nintendo DS came out. It had two screens. The bottom screen was a touch screen. Players used a **stylus** to select things on the screen!

Later that year, Sony released the PlayStation Portable, or PSP. It had a wide screen. Players could download games or use **UMDs**. These discs stored games or movies!

SO MANY GAMES

Between 2004 and 2014, more than 1,000 games were released for the PlayStation Portable. Popular games include *Daxter* and *Gran Turismo*.

HANDHELD GAMING
TODAY

Mario Kart 8 Deluxe on the Nintendo Switch

Today, Nintendo dominates handheld gaming. In 2017, the Nintendo Switch was released. It can be played both on a TV and as a handheld device. Favorite games include *Mario Kart 8 Deluxe* and *Animal Crossing: New Horizons*.

Nintendo also makes games for smartphones and tablets. The 2019 game *Mario Kart Tour* has millions of downloads!

Mario Kart Tour

RUN!
Super Mario Run is popular, too. The app has been downloaded over 300 million times!

Super Mario Run

Some **mobile** games were originally made for other devices. *Fortnite* was first made for computers and consoles in 2017. The next year, it was released as a mobile game!

Fortnite on mobile

POPULAR MOBILE GAMES
(BY NUMBER OF DOWNLOADS)

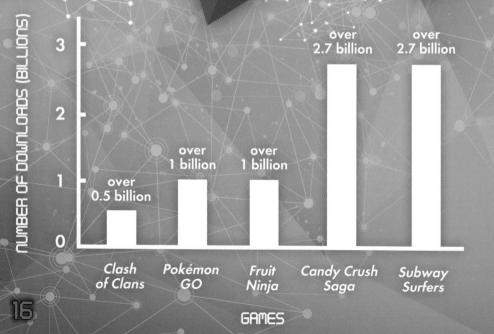

NUMBER OF DOWNLOADS (BILLIONS)

| | over 0.5 billion | over 1 billion | over 1 billion | over 2.7 billion | over 2.7 billion |

Clash of Clans | Pokémon GO | Fruit Ninja | Candy Crush Saga | Subway Surfers

GAMES

Other mobile games were originally made as **apps**. In 2009, the first Angry Birds game was released. Soon, more Angry Birds games were made. Today, Angry Birds games have been downloaded 4.5 billion times!

174 974

BIG-SCREEN BIRDS

Angry Birds has made it to the big screen! *The Angry Birds Movie* was released in 2016.

THE HANDHELD GAMING COMMUNITY

Clash Royale
tournament

Competitions are a big part of the handheld gaming community. Many players join **leagues**. In the league for the 2016 mobile game *Clash Royale*, ten teams compete to be the best!

Students can compete for **scholarships** in the High School **Esports** League. Many players use the Nintendo Switch. *Super Smash Bros. Ultimate* and *Rocket League* are commonly played!

High School Esports League competition

HANDHELD GAMING EVENT SPOTLIGHT

EVENT High School Esports League's Fall Major

WHEN IT HAPPENS once per year

WHERE IT HAPPENS United States

DESCRIPTION High school gamers compete in popular video games to earn money for college.

Larger events also allow people to celebrate and compete in handheld games. *Pokémon GO* players gather in cities around the world to catch special Pokémon. In 2018, an *Arena of Valor* championship had a $600,000 prize!

GAME SPOTLIGHT

GAME *Pokémon GO*

YEAR 2016

PLATFORM smartphones

DESCRIPTION Players search their real-life surroundings to find and train Pokémon and compete in gym battles.

Handheld gaming lets players take their favorite games almost anywhere. The handheld gaming community is full of fun!

Pokémon GO
gathering

GLOSSARY

apps—programs or games that can be downloaded onto mobile devices

cartridges—devices that hold the memory and graphics of games; cartridges are inserted into gaming devices.

competitions—events in which people are trying to win the same thing

esports—multiplayer video games that are played competitively for spectators

graphics—images displayed on a computer screen

grind—to slide along a surface on a skateboard

leagues—groups that come together to compete at a certain activity

mobile—relating to games that can be played almost anywhere on devices such as smartphones

obstacle—something that blocks movement or progress

scholarships—money given to students to help pay for further education

stylus—a pen-shaped tool used to write or touch buttons on a computer screen

UMDs—universal media discs; UMDs are small discs made for the PlayStation Portable that store the information for games and movies.

TO LEARN MORE

AT THE LIBRARY

Gregory, Josh. *History of Esports*. Ann Arbor, Mich.: Cherry Lake Publishing, 2020.

Hansen, Dustin. *Game On!: Video Game History from Pong and Pac-Man to Mario, Minecraft, and More*. New York, N.Y.: Feiwel & Friends, 2016.

Rathburn, Betsy. *Console Gaming*. Minneapolis, Minn.: Bellwether Media, 2021.

ON THE WEB

FACTSURFER

Factsurfer.com gives you a safe, fun way to find more information.

1. Go to www.factsurfer.com.

2. Enter "handheld gaming" into the search box and click Q.

3. Select your book cover to see a list of related content.

INDEX